Turning Back the Pages in... Old West Bridgford

............Dick Venner

Introduction

It is difficult to realise that in 1880 West Bridgford was a typical sleepy country village, with a population never much more than two hundred and fifty. The landscape was pasture and arable land, marsh, meadows and very few buildings of note. By 1895 the 'West Bridgford Estate' was very much a reality, developing the village with 'marvellous rapidity' into a recognisable semblance of the place of today.

That the village was to be developed into a residential estate, with many restrictions on the nature of commercial growth is best illustrated by the ban on public houses, which held force until 1936.

The postcards and snapshots reproduced in this book have been given to the library by local residents over a long period of time. They are all now kept at West Bridgford Library, where the collection can be seen and used at any time.

Nottinghamshire County Council
Community Services

West Bridgford Hall 1900

It was built by Mr Mundy Musters of Colwick Hall between 1768-1774. Mr Lewis Heymann took the lease c1841, and following his death in 1869 it was occupied by his son, Albert. He bought it from John Musters in 1883 and sold it to the Urban District Council in 1923. The residence is shown without Albert's later extensions, and gives a rare view of the Orangery.

The Hall in 1952, note the alterations, the clock and the remnants of the front bowling green, ruined by a bomb in 1941. This lawn was laid out for croquet in the 19th Century.

West Bridgford Hall Park possessed a small aviary in the 1920s and 30s, long since removed.

Rear of the Hall in 1952, with the lower tennis courts. An aspect which reinforces the unkind view of a building with little architectural distinction.

Opening celebrations of the Hall and the Park as public grounds in 1923.

Children's play area in West Bridgford Park, on the site of the future library, 1936.

West Bridgford Library situated close to the Hall, just prior to the official opening in 1939.

The Nottingham Journal 3rd March, 1939.

GOOD PUBLIC LIBRARIES

VIEW OF NOTTS. C.C. CHAIRMAN

AT BRIDGFORD

WHEN OPENING NEW BUILDING

REFERENCES to the value of libraries in helping to check the spread of "horrible Americanisms" were made by Major T. P. Barber (chairman of the Notts. County Council and Education Committee), when he opened West Bridgford's new library yesterday afternoon.

"We are beginning to think, eat, and drink American," he said. "I do think we shall forget how to speak our own language if we don't take a great deal of trouble."

Proceeding to talk of differing tastes, Major Barber said, as a youth, he used to read tuppenny dreadfuls. They were all about Red Indians, and he thought such books were often better than some of the "trash in modern novels."

He was often impelled to put some of the books he read on to the fire. Others he locked up so that people should not see them. Of modern books, he suggested the best for reading were historical novels.

PRINCIPAL WORTLEY

Principal H. A. S. Wortley (Chairman of the County Library Minor Sub-Committee), who presided, said very properly the opinion of the authorities of the Notts. County Council was that libraries and their work should be closely associated with the services of education.

One of the aims of education in school should be to develop in boys and girls —and later, in adults—a love of good books, and the habit of reading them intelligently.

We should not believe everything we read, but should read critically and constructively as well as destructively. A kind of "listening-in" or "passive reading" was very little use.

LED THE COUNTRY

One of the striking features of the library service was the great improvement in the qualifications of librarians, and he congratulated the County Librarian, Miss Austin, on the work she had done in conjunction with the County Libraries sub-committee.

In a letter from Mr. Arundell Esdaile (President of the Library Association), it was stated that the Notts. County Council were one of the earliest in the country to perceive the value of rural libraries, and to adopt the first effective scheme by which access to books should be no longer the privilege of dwellers in large towns.

In the last ten years, readers in the Notts. County libraries had multiplied by three and books by five.

After the opening, Major Barber "handed" the new library to Mr. J. W. Holmes (chairman of the West Bridgford Library Committee). Mr. Holmes and Mr. John Lawson (chairman of the West Bridgford Council) thanked the speakers.

The new library is a single storey building which comprises a lending and children's library, and study and reading rooms.

PROVISION FOR CHILDREN

It has cost about £6,200 and a further £1,045 has been expended on fittings.

The main walls are of sand faced bricks, and the facade and a central feature has dressings of natural Clipsham stone.

The building was designed by Mr. E. W. Roberts (county architect).

It was originally intended that no provision should be made for children from elementary schools, but the scheme was revised and provision is now made for children over 11 years of age.

The shelf capacity is 7,000 books and there is storage room for 6,000. The library opens with 10,000 volumes, which will be increased later.

In addition to a population of 21,000 in West Bridgford the library will serve library centres and schools within a range of five miles. Actually the total population served will eventually be about 31,500.

Nottm. Journal. 3. 3. 39

Peatfield Almshouses 1973 The commemorative stone reads 'These Almshouses were built by Mrs Catherine Peatfield, youngest daughter of Clifford and Catherine Caunt of West Bridgford, and widow of the Reverend John Peatfield, who was 29 years Curate in charge of this Parish. In the background is the embankment of the former Midland Railway line to Melton Mowbray (closed 1965).

Trent Bridge Police Station, 1870.

This stood near the old Bridge arch, close to the main road - well sited to supervise traffic and to intercept home bound poachers and other malefactors. It was in fact part of the City until 1952.

Wright's Directory of Nottingham 1905

URBAN DISTRICT COUNCIL.

Meets at the Board room, Public Elementary school, on the first friday in each month, at 8 p.m.

Chairman, W. J. Furse.

Vice-Chairman, W. R. Smart.

Retire April, 1906.

Alfred Dearnley	George T. Lovett
Henry Roe	George Hill
J. E. Shaw	

Retire April, 1907.

George Aylett	A. Heymann
Thomas Barlow	George T. Nelson
Jesse Gray	

Retire April, 1908.

Thomas Flewitt	William R. Smart
William J. Furse	Francis Stanhope
William Maggs	

Officers.

Clerk, William H. Redgate, Bentinck buildings, Wheeler gate, Nottingham

Treasurer, Henry E. Thornton, Union of London & Smiths Bank Limited, Nottingham

Medical Officer of Health, Walter Hunter M.B. Bridgeway house, 3 Arkwright street, Nottingham

Surveyor, Sanitary Inspector & Engineer, William Pare C.E. George road

Rate Collector, Thomas Crow Gray, 38 Millicent road

Police Station, Trent Bridge, Tom Stapleton, sergeant

PUBLIC ELEMENTARY SCHOOLS.

A committee of managers was formed in June, 1903, William Moss, Eldon chambers, Wheeler gate, Nottingham, correspondent

Higher Grade (mixed), opened in 1895, for 360 children; enlarged in 1897 & an additional building was added in 1902, for 600 children; average attendance, 600; Ernest J. Eley, master; Miss Edith N. Allen, infants' mistress

Trent boulevard (mixed), opened in 1899, for 314 children; average attendance, 300; Fred Foster, head master

(For names see under Nottingham.)

Sad remnants of the National School in August 1979. It was opened in 1865 and closed in 1900. The Conservative Club on Rectory Road is now on this site, and some of the original building can still be seen. The original architects were Hine and Evans of Nottingham.

Musters Road Schools 1979. First opened in April 1895, as a Board School, it changed name and was extended many times as the local population grew. Demolished in 1980, the site has been used for the new Health Centre.

South County School opened in 1914 on Exchange Road, first known as the South Council School. It started with 420 infant and junior children. This class, c1927, would seem to be the senior group.

George Road School, opened in 1902 by Lord Belper for 430 infant and junior children. Although a typical Board School, its design still fits the confident nature of local development. This class was pictured in 1920-22.

Lady Bay Infants School 1947-8

The school was opened in June 1899 as the Trent Boulevard Board School, expanded in 1905, and a new school built close by in 1912 for junior children.

Air Raid Precautions - WEST BRIDGFORD

A

CONCERT

will be given by the Co-ARP-timists in

The Musters Road Schools

ON

Thursday, May 23rd, 1940

at 7-30 p.m.

ARTISTES:

Miss M. Scarrott — Mr. H. E. Warth — Mr. H. Fletcher
Miss E. Minnett — Mr. J. C. Hutton — Mr. E. E. Nightingale
Mrs. D. M. Hughes — Pianist, Miss C. M. May
Producer, Mr. S. P. Goodyear Kettley. — Hon. Sec. Mrs. M. A. Honor

An appeal for Civil Defence Volunteers will be made by the Chairman of the Council, A. C. Flewitt, Esq., J.P., Chairman of A.R.P. Committee, W. Bralesford, Esq.; Assistant Sub-Controller A. C. Norman Smith, Esq., L.A.R.P.; and District Sub-Controller, R. C. S. Ross, F.A.R.P.I.

Residents over 16 years of age invited. — ADMISSION FREE

District Sub-Controller, West Bridgford

The Second World War brought hardship and suffering: none more so than the night of the 8th/9th May 1941. Sixty two H.E. bombs fell, with some fatalities and much damage. Trent Boulevard, the Park, Musters Road and the Cricket ground were all hit.

This picture shows the crater on the Bowling Green, which never recovered.

Post war, 1948, showing an Armistice Day service. In the top left can be seen one of the bomb sites, which was later used for the flats on Musters Road.

'Dad's Army'
performed valuable service on the Home Front. This inspection was at the Melton Road Brickworks in 1941.

Floods 1932

The River Trent has always been prone to flooding, with its catchment including the Peak District with its frequent snow melt. West Bridgford, being quite near the water level has suffered frequently, although the Embankment and Holme Sluice have reduced the flood risk to a considerable extent. 1932, 1946 and 1947 were all bad years, but many areas suffered almost annually.

May 1932 was the wettest for 160 years, with continuous heavy rain causing a huge rise in the water levels. West Bridgford fared particularly badly, as evidenced by these photographs, being completely marooned. Local boats were pressed into action ferrying people, goods and supplies. All sorts of transport were tried, although many vehicles were put out of action by the depth of the water.

Junction of Wilford Lane, Melton Road and Loughborough Road, looking up the latter. This ferry was often seen at flood episodes, being the only way to cross to higher and drier land.

Railway bridge on Bridgford Road.
Even in 1932 there were jams, and motorists could not bear to wait for a safe path. The bridge was widened soon after this, but the dip has never disappeared.

Melton Road 1932

Much more efficient, this steam wagon was ideal for towing stranded vehicles.

A view of Tudor Square, the Tudor Cinema and one of the oldest buildings, Church Farm, on the left. This was on Rectory Road, and was demolished in about 1970. It was one of the last remnants of the original village.

1947 Freeze and Flood. The winter of 1946/47 was one of the worse of the century, with snow starting to fall on 6th January, and the freezing conditions stayed with only brief intervals until the cataclysmic thaw on 16th March. The Trent burst its banks at Wilford, and Nottingham was pretty well cut off from the South and East. Four thousand homes were affected, and over twenty eight miles of streets were flooded and impassable. West Bridgford, perhaps for the last time, again became marooned.

Tudor Square in 1947, the shops have since been demolished to make way for the Barclays Bank building.

Tudor Square, looking down Central Avenue. Business somewhat less than brisk.

Abbey Road was obviously a favourite drive through shallow waters.

Musters Road at the junction with Rectory Road, 1947.

Loughborough Road by the Wolds Hotel, which was the high water mark for this flooding. 1947

Melton Road shops - again, a not surprising lack of trade. 1947

Sports in West Bridgford

West Bridgford has been a haven for sporting enthusiasts since William Clarke opened Trent Bridge Cricket Ground in 1839. Nottingham Forest moved to the south bank of the Trent in 1898, and all manner of boating clubs, football, tennis, cricket and bowling clubs came into being in and around the expanding community. After the Hall Park became public ground in 1923, it soon offered pay as you play facilities, and Sir Julien Cahn's cricket ground became the Memorial Park. The following photographs give a brief look into the leisure pursuits of a wealthy middle class community.

WEST BRIDGFORD URBAN DISTRICT COUNCIL

Spend Your Leisure Time in the
WEST BRIDGFORD PARK
Amid Delightful Surroundings

Every Facility For Healthy Outdoor Sports

TENNIS (Six Hard Courts)

THE COURTS ARE BOOKABLE PER HOUR

Doubles	**6d.** per hour per person
Singles	**9d.** ,, ,, ,, ,,
Juveniles—Morning and Afternoon Play Only	
Doubles	**3d.** per hour per person
Singles	**4½d.** ,, ,, ,, ,,

In addition, four "Griselda" hard courts are being constructed, and, at the time of the publication of this handbook, charges had not been fixed.

BOWLING GREENS (Two)

Afternoon	**4d.** per hour per person
Evening	**6d.** ,, ,, ,, ,,

Including use of Woods and Slippers.

CROQUET

6d. per hour per person. Hoops and balls provided but not mallets.

APPLICATION TO BE MADE TO PARK KEEPERS.

FOOTBALL (Two Pitches)

Pitches for organised games may be hired at the rate of 7s. 6d. per match. Dressing accommodation provided. Apply to Surveyor's Department at The Hall.

PLAYING FIELDS, WILFORD LANE

A cordial invitation to visit these spacious Playing Fields is given. They are of easy access and pleasantly situated and offer facilities for Summer and Winter Sports

Lady Bay was a much higher density development than the earlier estates, but even here the close proximity of the open land known as the Hook, by the river, allowed for plenty of healthy sporting activity. Thankfully it still does.

Trent Bridge Cricket Ground has often been used for unusual events down the years, and this ladies cycle demonstration, in the best possible taste, took place in 1903.

Trent Bridge Cricket Ground 1900. Probably an early morning view, given the shadows and the very sparse crowd.

The Laurels Tennis Club members enjoyed their games on the tennis courts on Rectory Road. Although undated, the costume surely dates from the 1920s. The Great War was still having its effect on the membership.

Before the advent of the Watersports Centre the Trent was even more crowded by leisure and sporting water activities than today. Nottingham Forest's ground was very small and the Boat Clubs were very active socially in the 1950s.

West Bridgford was a small rural village until 1881, with a fairly static population, pre-development, of 293 people. The 1881 census records fifty five dwellings. By 1914 the population was 13,476, and there were 3,369 houses. Traces of the original village still exist, but by the 1920s most had gone. What must the families of 1881 thought of this explosion of growth, and where did they go? The photographs on this page reflect the older West Bridgford, some being taken as part of a photographic survey of 1923 recording the buildings immediately prior to demolition.

The only pub in West Bridgford was the Trent Bridge Inn, then half in Nottingham, and serving the Cricket Club patrons. This photograph of the 1880s shows the original, long since redeveloped. The local Defence League successfully thwarted any further public house licence application until 1938, when the Wolds and the Test Match were begun.

copy of 1888 Directory entry

WEST BRIDGFORD is a parish, township and village, on the south bank of the river Trent, at the junction of the Grantham canal, 1½ miles south-by-east from Nottingham, the nearest station on the Nottingham and Melton Mowbray branch of the Midland railway, in the Rushcliffe division of the county, wapentake of Rushcliffe, Basford union, Nottingham petty sessional division, county court district and archdeaconry, rural deanery of West Bingham and diocese of Southwell. The church of St. Giles is an old stone building in the Early English style, and consists of chancel, nave, south aisle and south porch, with a square stone embattled tower at the east end, with pinnacles and 3 bells: the church was restored and seated with open pine benches in 1872: some of the windows contain fragments of ancient stained glass; a handsome carved oak rood screen of great antiquity separates the chancel from the nave: there is an ancient plain

DIRECTORY.] NOTTINGHAMSHIRE. WEST BRIDGFORD. 935

stone font and a modern wooden pulpit: the church plate consists of a chalice and paten (date 1809), also a cup (date 1659): there are 194 sittings, all free. The register dates from the year 1559 and is in fair condition. The living is a rectory, net yearly value £488, including 25 acres of glebe, in the gift of John P. Chaworth Musters esq. J.P. and held since 1862 by the Rev. William Roe Waters B.A. of Corpus Christi college, Cambridge. The parish shares in Dame Pierrepont's charity. Bridgford was a Roman settlement. In the Saxon times there was an extensive fortification erected here to prevent the passage across the Trent by the Danes, who, when in possession of Nottingham, attempted to pass over the Trent where the noble bridge crosses. In October, 1875, a great flood occurred here; the Trent overflowed its banks, and the village was many feet under water, much property being destroyed. Adjoining the Trent Bridge inn is the cricket ground, comprising 7 acres, with handsome pavilion, built by the County Cricket Club. John P. Chaworth Musters esq. J.P. who is lord of the manor and Mrs. Peatfield are the principal landowners. The soil is gravel; subsoil, clay. The chief crops are wheat, barley, oats and roots. The acreage is 1,720; rateable value, £9,973; the population in 1881, exclusive of Gamston, was 293.

GAMSTON is a township 1 mile east: it contains a portion of the hamlet of BASINGFIELD, the other portion thereof being in the parish of Holme Pierrepont, in the souther division of the wapentake of Bingham. The population is 95.

BURROWS HILL is half a mile north.

WALL LETTER BOX, at Mr. Walker's farmhouse, cleared at 7 p.m.; no post on sundays. Letters through Nottingham, which is the nearest money order & telegraph office, arrive at 7 a.m

School, now called a Church of England school, was endowed by the Rev. William Thompson with £27 yearly; it was rebuilt in 1865; William Stevenson, master

Photograph taken by J. R. Hammond

Rectory Road, c1923 The cottage on the right of the first picture was demolished soon after, but the other Church Farm, survived until 1970. It was on the plot now occupied by the Telephone Exchange, and, as evidenced by the second photograph, was in a very poor abandoned state in 1969.

This was not the last old Bridgford cottage, since at least three still exist in some part. It was the Stokes family farm, held on tenancy from the Musters family for at least six generations. It stood at the corner of Gordon Road and Blake Road, and was demolished in the 1920s. The lady was Mrs Stokes, who nursed in the village, and one of the children was William Stokes.

A rare view of the approach to Bridgford off Trent Bridge in 1932. The building on the right was the Police Station next to Mr Smart's house. Both fell victim to traffic schemes, although little evidence of the need for control can be seen. Mr Smart, who died in 1933, was on the Local Government Board.

The former line of Arkwright Street and its junction with London Road can clearly be seen, with the empty reservoir of the Trent Waterworks to the left.

View of the Meadows over the Reservoir. More houses and at least 4 more roads swallowed up the empty acreage between 1901 and 1910.

Taken from the top of the Town Arms

These magnificent photographs are from a diorama
taken from the top of the Town Arms in 1898.
The new Nottingham Forest Ground is seen,
with crowds crossing the then narrow Trent Bridge
on their way to a match.
Witty's Boat Builders are in operation, with
two of the steam boats built at the yard.
County Hall does not exist, and cricket pitches
and Lovers Walk stetch along an
unconfined River Trent.
The haze hides the many gaps in the built up
areas, since development continued to 1914 and beyond

Trent Bridge in 1898 was much narrower, as can be seen. Lover's walk and the playing fields now occupied by County Hall were favourite summer walks originally known as Aldermen's Parts, the fields were allotments in earlier years.

A view of a thriving commercial and recreational river. Nottingham Forest have reached their current home, and the Boat Clubs, and Witty's Boatyards are thriving. Two of the Witty built steamers are shown.

Turney Brothers Factory was built c1875. Sir John Turney lived at Adbolton Hall, and was Sheriff and Mayor (twice) of Nottingham. He was a member of the Corporation for 46 years.

Shows the early beginnings of the Victoria Embankment and the now disused Trent Waterworks Engine Pumphouse.

The Buses

As West Bridgford grew, so did the need for bus services. At first firms like Thos. Clarke of Exchange Road, and W Bamford & Sons gave residents a good choice, but in 1914 the Urban District Council (U.D.C.) began its own services. During the next 50 years the services changed and developed, often due to the competition of 'pirate' companies, especially in the 1920s. Initially passengers had to change at Trent Bridge but through routes began to be initiated from 1928. The undertaking was finally sold to the Corporation in 1968.

SANDS'S WEST BRIDGFORD. 105

BUSES

Run every Half-hour. Fares 1d.

Between St. Peter's Square & Musters Road, Bridgford.

First Bus from Musters Road, 7.55 a.m.; last, 10.25 p.m.
First ,, ,, St. Peter's Sq., 8.25 a.m.; last, 10.55 p.m.

Also every Half-hour :—
First Bus from Musters Road, 8.10 a.m.; last, 9.40 p.m.
First ,, ,, St. Peter's Sq., 8.40 a.m.; last, 10.10 p.m.

SUNDAYS.

First Bus from Musters Road, 5.55 p.m.; last, 9.55 p.m.
First ,, ,, St. Peter's Sq., 6.25 p.m.; last, 10.15 p.m.

Horse bus on Musters Road, c1910. The elegant driver was Bertie Wainwright, who always wore a button-hole flower, and was most helpful and cheery.

Horse bus on Charnwood Grove c1890. Run by Nottingham and District Tramways, and travelling at a pace which must have pleased the advertisers.

U.D.C. bus on Melton Road, c1918.

Route 21 to Edwalton had the newest buses as seen in this example in 1964.

One of the last U.D.C. Buses, followed by one of its successors, on Loughborough Road near the Gem supermarket in 1968.

Rails, Rivers, Canals

West Bridgford owes its existence to the river crossing, the roads leading to it, and to the Bridge. The river, its floods and its amenities is a constant in the life of the community. To a lesser extent the Grantham Canal and the railways had a physical impact on the design of the expansion estates. No station was allowed, however - to lessen any undesirable influx of visitors although there were goods sidings at Smart's Yard which is now Ludlow Hill commercial estate.

Railway Bridge over Melton Road - this carried the fast line to London via Melton Mowbray. The bridge was demolished 18/19 January 1975. Photo taken February 1974 by Reg Baker.

Steam locomotive passing Smart's Siding - picture taken 30 May 1955.

Musters Road Railway embankment, August 1959. Pure heaven for the train spotter, but a somewhat noisy neighbour.

The old swing bridge over the Grantham Canal leading to Rutland Road. Known locally as the Meccano Bridge, it was demolished in 1953.

The Canal and a strangely quiet Radcliffe Road, taken in 1950. The old canal cottage can just be seen on the left.

The frozen Trent in February 1895. A sight that will probably never be seen again, unless the Power Stations cease to use water.

The original church of St Giles rapidly became insufficient for the rapidly growing community and its many denominations. All Hallows was opening in 1889 and rebuilt in 1908. The Friary Congregational Church opened in 1901, Musters Road Weslyan Church opened in 1899, and the Baptist Church in 1907. Trent Boulevard Methodist Church was erected in 1901, but the Gordon Road Methodist Church was never built, services being held in the Church Hall built in 1927.

Before the rapid expansion of the village from 1881, St Giles was the major place of worship. A small church dating from the early thirteenth century. Restored in 1871, it was enlarged in 1898 and in 1911.
This photo was taken prior to the original restoration.

Musters Road and the Friary Church pictured in 1916.

FRIARY CONGREGATIONAL CHURCH, MUSTERS ROAD

SANDS'S WEST BRIDGFORD. 37

Friary Congregational Church,

MUSTERS ROAD.

Minister :—REV. W. E. PERFECT, M.A.
Sunday Services :—10-45 a.m. and 6-30 p.m.
Sunday School :—2-30.

The Congregational Church Hymnal is used.

The stones of the School were laid on Tuesday, September 13th, 1898, by the late J. N. Dunn, Esq., and the School was opened for temporary worship in March, 1899, when the Rev. W. E. Perfect, M.A. commenced his ministry.

The memorial stones of the Church were laid on Thursday, September 20th, 1900, by Miss E. S. M. Peat, Mr. W. Lee, J.P., and Mr. J. G. Watts, and the Church was opened for worship the following year, Tuesday, September 24th, 1901. The style is late Gothic, constructed of white stone known as Coxbench, with Ancaster and Derbyshire dressings, and a tower rises at the corner of Musters Road

THE PARISH CHURCH

OF

ALL HALLOWS - LADY BAY

LADY BAY CHURCH — 1906

"A Jubilee shall that fiftieth year be unto you."
—Lev. 25, 11

———: o :———

Golden Jubilee Commemoration

———: o :———

7 p.m. FRIDAY, 9th NOVEMBER, 1956

———: o :———

From the first West Bridgford was unlike many other developments in that very few industrial or retail sites were to be allowed. The sale plans perhaps spell out the original reasons. To keep the area both residential and almost exclusive Mr Musters stipulated that no building erected on any of the lots should be used as a factory or worksop. No slaughter house or pigsty was allowed, nor was any noxious, noisy or offensive trade to be carried out. No public house, beer house or club house, or indeed any off-licence was to be allowed either.

Industry and commerce was mostly held at bay until the late 1930s, excepting minor trades in Lady Bay.

The first shop to be built on Central Avenue was the Post Office and General Stores in 1892, and the Avenue was finally cut through the croft to Rectory Road in 1900.

There were five corner shops and bakeries by 1906, and retail developments in Musters Road and Radcliffe Road were house conversions in 1904 and 1912.

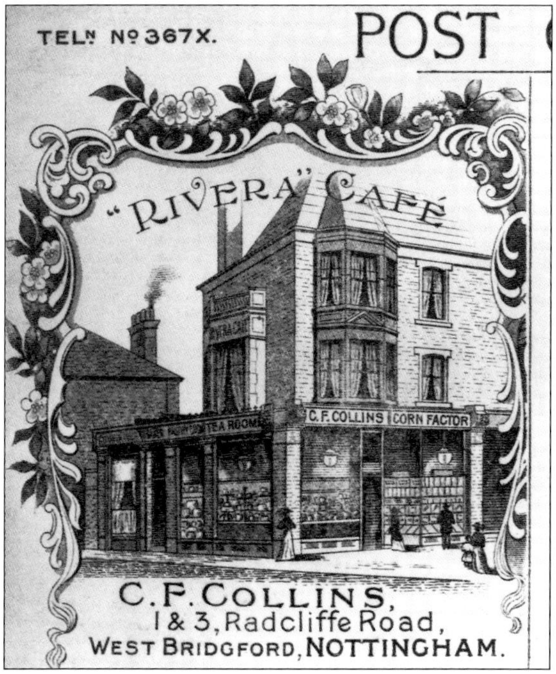

C. F. Collins shop and 'Rivera' Cafe in 1900. The first Chess Club met here in the 1890s.

The Midlands Industrial Exhibition, with fair ground, only lasted for two years. It burnt down soon after this picture was taken in 1904. Again, this stood on the much used Civic Centre site.

Melton Road Garage, 1935. A very small retail area at this time, and none of the houses on the left had been converted into shops.

WELDING CELLULOSE SPRAYING
HIGH PRESSURE GREASING
WING REPAIRS
CAR WASHING

Have your car overhauled during the winter months. Let us quote you for re-boring, de-carbonising, etc.

All Repairs Carried Out by Expert Mechanics and Fully Guaranteed

LARGE STOCKS OF TYRES & ACCESSORIES

Lady Bay Garage

(Proprietor — S. H. STEPHENSON, M.I.M E.)

RADCLIFFE ROAD
WEST BRIDGFORD

Telephone 84971

1927 - Central Avenue - with the recently built shopping block. It didn't take long for the pavements to be 'dug up' - a true twentieth century phenomenon.

Central Avenue and the Tudor Cinema in 1950. Parking was a problem even then.

The one time industrial site, the Melton Road Brickyard in 1952. In the 1890s this was leased by Mr W R Smart of Stratford Road, who later moved to the house next to the Police Station on Trent Bridge. The area is now the Ludlow Hill Industrial Park.

Loughborough Road, 1957, next to the Wolds Hotel. Collington's Farm was redeveloped as the Gem supermarket, later Asda.

Directory entry

WEST BRIDGFORD is a parish, township and village, on the south bank of the river Trent, at the junction of the Grantham canal, 1½ miles south-by-east from Nottingham, the river being here crossed by a substantial bridge; the parish is in the Rushcliffe division of the county, wapentake of Rushcliffe, Basford union, Nottingham petty sessional division, county court district and archdeaconry, rural deanery of West Bingham and diocese of Southwell. By an Order of the County Council, confirmed by Local Government Board Order No. 26,979, dated 16 July, 1891, a Local Board was established for West Bridgford, but under the provisions of the "Local Government Act, 1894" (56 and 57 Vict. c. 73), this has been superseded by an Urban District Council. The church of St. Giles is an ancient building of stone in the Early English style, consisting of chancel, nave, north and south aisles, lady chapel, vestries, south porch and an embattled tower at the east end, with pinnacles and containing 3 bells: the north aisle, lady chapel and vestries were added in 1912 at a cost of over £5,000: the church was restored and seated with open pine benches in 1872; some of the windows contain fragments of ancient stained glass; a handsome carved oak rood screen of great antiquity separates the chancel from the nave; there is an ancient but plain stone font and a modern wooden pulpit: the church plate consists of a chalice and paten dated 1809, and a cup dated 1659: in 1898 the church was completely restored and a new nave and chancel erected at a cost of £6,000: there are now 800 sittings. The register dates from the year 1559 and is in fair condition. The living is a rectory, net yearly value £500, with 4 acres of glebe and residence, in the gift of J. C. Waddington esq. and Mrs. Robinson, and held since 1904 by the Rev. Richard Hargreaves M.A. of Corpus Christi College, Cambridge. The Memorial Mission church, in South fields, is a small iron building. An iron church was erected in 1891 on the Lady Bay estate, at a cost of £500. Here is a Catholic church, dedicated to the Sacred Heart. The Wesleyan chapel, Musters road, erected in 1899, is of stone, and will seat 800. The Baptist chapel, in Melton road, erected in 1907, at a cost of £5,000, is a building of stone, and will seat 560. Six almshouses were built in 1892 by Mrs. Catherine Peatfield, youngest daughter of Clifford and Catherine Gaunt, of West Bridgford, and widow of the Rev. John Peatfield, who was 29 years curate of this parish. The parish shares in Dame Pierrepont's charity. Bridgford was a Roman settlement. In the Saxon times extensive fortifications were constructed here to prevent the incursion of the Danes. Adjoining the Trent Bridge inn is a cricket ground of 7 acres, with a pavilion, built by the County Cricket Club. West Bridgford Hall is the residence of Albert Heymann esq. D.L., J.P. Col. Davies and Miss Peatfield are the principal landowners. The soil is gravel; subsoil, clay. The chief crops are wheat, barley, oats and roots. The area is 1,116 acres of land and 7 of water; rateable value, £69,341; the population, exclusive of Gamston, in 1901 was 6,797. The population of the Urban District in 1901 was 7,018 and of the ecclesiastical parish, 7,098, and in 1911, Urban Dstrict, 11,632, and ecclesiastical parish, 11,722, and 1921, 13,352.

URBAN DISTRICT COUNCIL.

Meets at the Board Room, Public offices, Bridgford road, on the 2nd friday in each month, at 7 p.m.

Officers.

Clerk, William Herbert Redgate, Bentinck buildings, 15 Wheeler gate, Nottingham

Treasurer, Bertram Abel Smith, The National Union & Provincial Bank of England Limited, Nottingham

Medical Officer of Health, Walter Hunter M.D. 6 Bridgford road, West Bridgford

Surveyor & Sanitary Inspector, William Pare C.E. Bridgford road, Nottingham

District Rate Collector, Robert Percy Simons, 1 Radcliffe road, West Bridgford

---

Public Elementary Schools.

A committee of managers was formed in June, 1903: Ernest H. B. Slade, 59 Seymour road, West Bridgford, correspondent

West Bridgford Secondary School, Musters road (mixed), opened in 1895, for 360 children; enlarged in 1897 & an additional building was added in 1902, for 600 children; F. B. Davies B.A. head master

Trent Boulevard (mixed), opened in 1912, for 320 children; Jesse Gray, master

GAMSTON (or South Gamston) is a hamlet in the civil parish of West Bridgford and ecclesiastical parishes of Holme Pierrepont and West Bridgford. It is 3 miles south from Nottingham, in the Newark division of the county, northern division of Bingham wapentake, Basford union and Bingham county court district. Earl Manvers is sole landowner The chief crops are wheat, barley, oats, clover and roots. The area is 448 acres; rateable value, £722; the population in 1911 was 74.

Letter Box

Letters arrive from Radcliffe-on-Trent. Radcliffe road, West Bridgford, 1½ miles distant, is the nearest money order & telegraph office

The children of this hamlet attend the school at Holme Lane

The Urban District Council run a service of motor omnibuses every few minutes from Trent Bridge to all parts of West Bridgford

For names in both places see under Nottingham.

Victorian Elegance, Fox and Hound Road c1900

Part of the early development, and named after the pack of foxhounds kept by Mr Musters at Colwick Hall.

The new and old Trent Bridge Inns

Smarts Brickyard workers wait with their transport for Mr Smart to send off the Annual Outing.

Trent Boulevard and its bus transport in 1909. The road was forty feet wide, and built up above the surrounding land to help avoid flooding.

Lady Bay Bridge in 1914

The main Radcliffe Road swings to the right. No trace now remains.

Priory Road in 1913 - at this date a very short road, not completed until the 1930s.

Radcliffe Road, near Pavilion Road c1952.

A leafy view of Central Avenue in 1950

Jubilee celebrations in Tudor Square, 1935

Crosby Road in the 1920s No parking problems. Most of these houses were built in 1906.

The roads leading to Trent Bridge in 1920. A busy , but strangely peaceful scene, with the emphasis on people.

Rectory Road 'The Poplars' 1960 This was owned by Clifford Caunt, one of the two major landowners in old West Bridgford. His daughter, Catherine Peatfield, occupied it after his death, and it was she who erected the Peatfield Almshouses. Soon after this picture was taken the house was demolished, although the name continues on the current block of flats occupying this site.

The old Rectory, Church Drive, c1920 Although this was not the first on the site, it was a traditionally over large house, very expensive to run and difficult to heat. It was demolished c1965, replaced by a neat modern edifice, itself demolished when the site was sold. A long history of church ownership has now come to an end.

A view of the Trent Bridge approaches in 1956, shortly before redevelopment and the demolition of the two buildings on the left.

Acknowledgements

Many of the earlier photographs have been copied from original postcards. The compiler wishes to thank the many local residents of West Bridgford who have donated photographs. Known attributions being Alan Bailey (p. 38 lower), Reg Baker (p. 5, p. 6 and p. 22 all upper), John Hammond (p .19 lower and p. 22 lower), Peter Hammond (p. 22 lower and p. 38 lower), J. W. Mitchell (p. 12 upper and p.13 lower), E. Richardson (p. 14 upper), Mr Collington (P. 44 lower) and Mr. John Wilson (P. 35 upper).

The text on page 6 and photographs on pages 9 (lower), 11 (upper), and 52 have been attributed to the Nottingham Evening Post and their permission to reproduce them here is gratefully acknowledged.

ISBN 0 902751 37 9